Attending to Scripture

A Course of Six Bible Studies on How we Read the Bible

Jonathan Baker

Vicar of Scalby and Hackness with Harwood Dale

GROVE BOOKS LIMITED
RIDLEY HALL RD CAMBRIDGE CB3 9HU

Contents

1. Introduction 3
2. Images of the Word 8
3. The People of the Book: Nehemiah 8.1–12 10
4. The Authority of Scripture: 2 Timothy 3.10–4.5 14
5. Meditating on God's Word: Psalm 1 18
6. Christ the Key to the Scriptures: Acts 8.26–40 21
7. Entering God's Story: Luke 24.13–491 24
8. For Further Reading 28

Acknowledgements

I would like to thank members of the Grove Spirituality Group who read and made helpful comments on an early draft of this booklet, and especially Graham Pigott, Roly Riem, Ian Silk and Alison White. Thanks are also due to the people of St Laurence's, Scalby; St Peter's, Hackness; St Margaret's, Harwood Dale and Scalby Methodist Church who first tried out these studies and encouraged me to write them up. Finally, this booklet is dedicated to the people of York Diocese, who are committed together to 'attending to God in worship, prayer, and the study of the Scriptures.'

The Cover Illustration is by Peter Ashton

Copyright © Jonathan Baker 2002

First Impression February 2002
ISSN 0262-799X
ISBN 1 85174 490 8

1
Introduction

What is the difference between reading the Bible and hearing the word of God? The question may sound provocative. Surely when we read the Bible we *are* hearing the word of God?

I have no intention of reviewing different doctrines of Scripture or theories of biblical inspiration and interpretation. My concern is a practical one. It stems from the simple observation that when most Christians read the Bible or hear it read we do not experience it as the word of God. That is, when the lessons are read out in church, or verses quoted by preachers, or passages referred to in books, all too often we do not find ourselves being nourished in our spirits. There is a great gap between what is claimed for the Bible and the way we actually experience it. I suggest that this gap is the main reason why so many Christians do not see the Bible as essential for their spiritual growth.

No doubt all believers see the Bible as a useful source of information containing the details of Israel's history or Jesus' ministry. Probably most Christians regard it as having some sort of authority when discussing Christian life and behaviour. Many of us believe it ought to be the wellspring of our faith. But how many people encounter the Bible in practice as the basic resource of the spiritual life? How many see it not just as a badge of evangelical identity, but as a point of meeting with God where faith can be renewed and intimacy deepened? And how many struggle with guilt because they believe this ought to be their experience, yet find that it eludes them? All too often when we turn to the Bible, perhaps driven there by a gnawing spiritual hunger to hear a word of life, what we actually encounter is an ancient, dry and alien text, in some places as offensive as it is unfathomable. It seems the rope on our bucket is too short to reach the water in the well—if water there be.

And yet the Bible itself has something to say about this. The author of Deuteronomy 6 is fully aware of the danger of forgetfulness as he passionately commends the practice of memorizing Scripture (including the use of any available *aide-memoir*!). And from 2 Kings 22 and Nehemiah 8 it is clear that God's word can all too easily be forgotten by the whole worshipping community. What is equally clear is the remarkable power of God's word to transform the same forgetful people when they turn to Scripture afresh.

In the Bible itself we find a wide range of ways of engaging with the Scriptures. For example, we might recognize something of the modern preacher in Paul when he urges upon Timothy a professional approach to

Scripture, like a workman who 'correctly handles the word of truth' (2 Timothy 2.15). To many, that will conjure an approach to the Bible which is responsible, scholarly and measured. But how does that stand alongside the prophet Ezekiel literally feeding on the word of God in a most unscholarly way, as he digests a scroll given by the Lord as a prelude to delivering its message to the house of Israel (Ezekiel 3.1–4)? The implication is clearly that God's word must be received at a gut level before it can be articulated. The word of God is not an object to be analysed and dissected so much as a banquet to be devoured as a token of love!

We all need help in coming to Scripture not as spectators curious to know what it contains, nor as pupils seeking information or guidance, nor even as critics seeking to interrogate the text and discover its truth, but as lovers seeking Christ himself. It is not that other approaches are wrong or misguided, but on their own they are not likely to help us in hearing the text as the word of God.

If the Bible is the word of God then people of all backgrounds and educational abilities must feel confident about reading it and being blessed by it. For this to happen, only two principles are essential. Firstly, the Bible must be read in the light of our Christian faith, and as the principal means of nourishing a living faith in Christ. Secondly, the Bible must be read in the context of the Christian community, not by isolated individuals who do not see themselves as part of the body of Christ. Such a minimalist approach doubtless allows room for all sorts of crude and unsophisticated interpretations; but it also allows people the freedom to hear the word of God speak with power and freshness on their own terms, and not always mediated by academics and clergy.

The aim of this booklet is therefore simply to offer encouragement and help to those who want to find spiritual nourishment in the Bible. It does this by taking several passages in which the biblical writers' own attitudes to Scripture are revealed. Each chapter offers some introductory comments about each passage and the issues it raises for our theme (to be read before the passage itself) and some questions for group discussion or individual reflection after reading the passage. In order to encourage an imaginative, emotional and practical engagement with the text, there are also prayers and a meditation on each passage. The material can be adapted and used selectively or creatively depending on the needs of each particular group.

Word of God?

Since we often call Scripture the 'word of God,' it might be helpful to acknowledge that the phrase can be used in the Bible in several related but distinct senses.

i) Jesus Christ is supremely the living Word through whom God's nature is revealed most fully, as several key New Testament passages make clear (for example John 1.1–14, Hebrews 1.1–2). The Word is consequently a Person, not a page, and can be 'heard' not primarily through intellectual understanding and assent, but through a personal response of commitment and faith developing into a relationship of trust and love. This relationship then becomes the context in which God's word is heard.

ii) The 'word of God' can also mean the same as 'gospel.' It is the proclaimed message of what God has actually done through the life, death and resurrection of Jesus. It is used in this way, for example, in Acts 6.7 and 1 Thessalonians 2.13. In Matthew's account of the parable of the sower, the seed is the 'message of the kingdom' (Matthew 13.19).

iii) There are places in the Bible where the very words of God are given in direct speech, as for example on Sinai (Exodus 20.1), or when the prophets say 'Thus says the Lord' (Isaiah 1.2, 10, 18, 24, and almost any passage of prophetic utterance). Red-letter Bibles, which print the words of Jesus in a different colour, reflect an understanding of 'the word of God' as literal speech.

iv) By extension, the whole Bible is the word of God, in the sense that it bears witness to the God and Father of our Lord Jesus Christ in an authoritative way and explores the implications of Christ's coming for all who believe in him. Jesus himself used the Old Testament Scriptures in this way, and there is plenty of evidence that the apostolic church used the New Testament writings similarly (for example Luke 4.4–12, John 20.31, 2 Timothy 3.15–16).

Beginning Bible Study

When looking for a way into any passage of Scripture, I find that there are some general questions which can be relied upon to yield a fruitful engagement with God's word. Whilst there is nothing original about these techniques, I set out below three sets of questions which may be of value as a reminder of how we can come to Scripture expecting it to make a difference to our whole lives.

My first approach is simply to ask:
1. What does this passage say about God?
2. What does this passage say about us in relation to God?
3. What does this passage say about the wider world in relation both to God and ourselves?

The second approach invites different levels of response:
1. Is there anything in this passage which speaks to my head, offering fresh insight or deepening my understanding?

2. Is there anything in this passage which touches my heart, stimulating my imagination, stirring my emotions or evoking my adoration?
3. Is there anything in this passage which releases my hands, inspiring me to action or challenging me to make some change in my life?

The final set of questions runs as follows:
1. Does the passage contain any warning to heed?
2. Does the passage contain any command to obey?
3. Does the passage contain any promise to claim?
4. Does the passage contain any example to follow?
5. Does the passage contain any word or phrase to memorize?
6. Does the passage contain anything which prompts me to pray?

By using such 'all-purpose' questions we may often find that we are provided with rich materials for prayer and adoration, as well as for practical action.

Bible reading can never be divorced from prayer; we cannot expect God to address us if we are not willing to give him our attention and response. It is therefore not enough simply to interrogate the text with the right questions. We must so dispose our hearts that God can be received.

How can this be done? Firstly, by reading attentively. This is difficult, because most of our reading is superficial. When we look at a printed page we are used to scanning it swiftly for information, gleaning what is of immediate interest and skipping the rest. By contrast, when we read the Bible we need to be alert but unhurried so that we are consciously reading in the presence of God. It is a form of reading which involves not just the eyes and the mind, but our whole being—emotions, intellect, imagination, conscience and will, so that we not only read the text but allow ourselves to be read by it.

This kind of reading can naturally flow into meditation, as we ruminate on a passage, going back over it, turning it over in our mind, savouring it. There may be a word or phrase we particularly want to hold on to and return to through the day, allowing it to surface every so often so that our spirits can gulp in fresh air. Such meditation moves us on from merely reading the word of God to receiving it and making it our own.

Reading and meditation then lead to prayer. We know that the word of God is beginning to take root in our hearts when we can take God's word to us and turn it around, repeating to God what he has said to us. Some parts of the Bible, such as the Psalms, invite such use. This, of course, is a principle which underlies the use of liturgy, for liturgy is a way of using Scripture in worship. Naturally, the Bible can also move us to pray in a wider sense, as our reading and meditation may prompt us to praise God for his mighty acts revealed in Scripture, and may move us to pray for God's involvement in the world and in our own lives.

As we read, meditate and pray, we shall often feel a dawning sense of God's presence. Not always, of course, and certainly not predictably, but often enough to remind us that the Bible can pull our lives into closer alignment with God. Occasionally we may reach a point where we simply want to adore our Lord in wordless silence, the words having done their essential work of bringing us to the living Word, Jesus himself.

Bible reading can then become a form of worship, in which we surrender ourselves to God with the aim of growing in intimacy with him. It is not too much to say that Scripture used in this way becomes a sacrament in which Christ himself is received.

When Scripture is received sacramentally, it will generate energy for spiritual change. Real worship helps to mould worshippers more in the likeness of Christ, and ultimately this is worked out not in the sanctuary but in the world. Consequently these studies include not only prayers and devotional material, but also encouragement to turn our hearing of the word into doing. In this way the Bible is not only a resource for faith and worship, but is also an engine of God's kingdom as it inspires deeper dissatisfaction with the world's priorities and a stronger desire to implement a genuinely Christian vision for our lives and for society.

2
Images of the Word

When the Bible refers to itself (usually preferring to speak of either 'the Scriptures' or 'the word of God') it often does so using a metaphor. These word-pictures are simple but vivid, and invite further reflection. Not least, they prompt us as we open our Bibles to ask the question, 'What kind of book have we got here?'

Preparatory Prayer
>   As your word, O Lord, gives light to our path,
>   may we behold the glory of your presence
>   and so rejoice to sing your praise,
>   now and for ever. Amen. (From *Celebrating Common Prayer*)

Questions for Discussion
   Before you go any further, you might like to consider your general attitude to the Bible.

- How do you feel about the Bible?
- Do you approach it as a challenge or a chore?
- Does the thought of it inspire numbness or excitement?
- Why do you read it (or feel you ought to read it)?
- What do you expect to gain from reading the Bible?

Your response to these questions will probably depend upon your past experience of the Bible. So think back and ask yourself the following:

- When did you start to read the Bible, and what led you to do it?
- How did your early experiences of the Bible shape the way you feel about it now?
- Has any passage troubled you or oppressed you, and made you wish it was not there?
- What passage do you remember best?
- What is it about it that speaks to you?

Below is a list of words and images which the Bible itself uses to describe God's word. Turning to your neighbour, play the word association game in which you read the list of images and your neighbour responds to each word by saying the first word he or she can associate with it. Then reverse roles.

IMAGES OF THE WORD

Afterwards, share why each of you made the associations you did.

Counsellor	Psalm 119.24
Fire	Deuteronomy 5.23–26, Jeremiah 23.29
Food	Ezekiel 2.9–3.3, Jeremiah 15.16, Psalm 119.103
God-breathed	2 Timothy 3.16
Hammer	Jeremiah 23.29
Inheritance	Psalm 119.111
Lamp	Psalm 119.105, Proverbs 6.23
Life	John 6.68, Philippians 2.16
Light	Psalm 119.105, 2 Peter 1.19
Mirror	James 1.22–26
Rod and staff	Psalm 23.4
Seed	Luke 8.11, 1 Peter 1.23
Sword	Ephesians 6.17, Hebrews 4.12, Revelation 1.16
Truth	John 17.17

Which of these images most attracts you? Do you find any of them surprising? Consider how you might read the Bible differently according to which image you have in mind.

Meditation
Read the following:

> The words of the Lord are pure words,
>   like silver refined from ore
>   and purified seven times in the fire.   (Psalm 12.6)

Lord, I thank you for the purity of your word. May it cleanse my soul, and draw me towards holiness.

Thank you for the light of your word. May it shine through my blindness and show me the way.

Thank you for the truth of your word. May it touch my mind, and reveal to me your glory.

Thank you for the seed of your word. May it take root in my heart, and grow and bear fruit.

Thank you for the fire of your word. May it burn within me and consume all my unbelief.

Thank you for the blade of your word. May it cut through my self-deception and guard me from evil.

Thank you for the reflection of your word. May it reveal what is hidden and show me my true self.

Thank you for the nourishment of your word. May it help me to grow and become strong in faith.
Thank you for the comfort of your word. May it give me patience and sustain my hope in you.

Action
Read a familiar passage repeatedly over a period of days, each time approaching it with a different word picture in mind. Notice how different insights are given depending on whether you are reading the passage as a 'mirror' or a 'hammer' and so on.

3
The People of the Book: Nehemiah 8.1–12

Comment
Whenever families gather together, it is likely that before very long people who have not seen each other for a while will start to reminisce.

'Do you remember old "Bunny" Hare at school? Whatever happened to him?'
'Do you remember that dreadful winter when the pipes burst and we couldn't get the car out of the drive?'
'Do you remember the night we first met and I couldn't remember your name?'

The sharing of memories is important because it reinforces our feelings of belonging to a particular group. Sometimes there is an older member of the family who loves to recount the defining family memories. Everyone knows about some incidents in the life of a family even if they were not there, because the memories are frequently repeated. My children seem to be more familiar with some episodes from my childhood than I am, because my mother will often recall them, and they are no longer my memories or hers, but belong firmly in the domain of the wider family.

The Bible can serve a similar purpose in creating a sense of belonging to God's family. It contains the core memories of the people of God, the events which have touched us all but which we easily forget have made us the people we are. It is not unlike the family photograph album, only the events are recorded in words instead of pictures. What is more, they have been given in order to be shared in the setting of a community.

In this passage we meet an entire nation which has forgotten its identity, and we see it making a concerted effort to reconnect with its spiritual roots by listening to the Scriptures. The Book of Nehemiah describes how the Jewish exiles returned from captivity in Babylon at the very end of the Old Testament period in about 450 BC. Unfortunately they had been away from home for so long and had so acclimatized to life in Babylon that their sense of being the covenant people of God, called out from the nations, had been severely weakened.

Here we see the exiles reconnecting with their pre-exilic identity by listening to the Book of the Law of Moses. Whether this was the completed Pentateuch (the first five books of the Bible) or one of the earlier strands of tradition which was later incorporated into the Pentateuch we do not know. What is clear is the tremendous power of this written tradition to re-invigorate the nation with a fresh awareness of its unique identity and calling. We read in this text the account of a remarkable transformation. No longer is the nation dependent upon its unchanging physical institutions such as the land, the Temple, and the monarchy. Neither does it continue to drift in amnesia and semi-exile, inhabiting the ancient homeland but unsure of its identity and calling. Instead the Law of Moses becomes the wellspring from which the renewal of Judaism flows. It was a crucial moment when the self-understanding of God's people shifted momentously and they were reborn as the 'people of the Book.'

Preparatory Prayer

Lord God, the source of truth and love,
keep us faithful to the apostles' teaching and fellowship,
united in prayer and the breaking of bread,
and one in joy and simplicity of heart,
in Jesus Christ our Lord. Amen.   (From *Common Worship*)

Questions for Discussion

1. Do you recognize in your own life or in that of the church the Israelites' sense of dislocation, of having forgotten who they truly were? What contributes towards such a feeling, and what might be the symptoms of such forgetfulness?
2. What have been the defining moments in the history of your local church? What gives your church its special ethos and sense of identity? How is that identity reinforced and handed on? How far is your own identity bound up with that of your church? Does your church have a calling?

3. Consider the relative merits of simply reading the word of God (v 3) as against hearing it preached (v 8). Why do we need both? How far does your faith depend upon other people? What help is available to help us understand the Bible?

Meditation
Read, slowly, James 1.23–25. Leave a period of silence.

Imagine that you wake up one morning, get up and go to the bathroom to wash. Imagine your surprise as you look in the mirror and see that it has turned opaque. It no longer reflects the image of your face. You try to remember what you look like, and think that you have a pretty clear recollection of your appearance. But when you come to put on your makeup or to shave you realize how unreliable your memory is. Imagine then going for days, months or even years without ever seeing the reflection of your face. What would that do to the way you think about yourself? What doubts might arise in your mind? How far does your self-confidence and self-image depend upon being able to picture yourself visually? Then, one day, without warning, you pass a mirror and realize with a shock that you can see yourself for the first time in ages. You turn and look into the mirror more carefully, and are shocked to see a face staring back at you which is almost that of a stranger. It dawns on you that in fact you look quite different from the way you remember.

Now consider a different situation. Imagine that your origins are unknown and that you were adopted as a baby. All you know about your natural parents is that they come from a different ethnic background to that of your adoptive parents. Your adoptive parents are kind and loving and have done their best to accept you fully as one of their children. But as you reach adulthood you are more and more aware that you do not fully belong and that part of your identity lies somewhere else. You have no knowledge of who your natural parents are or how to find them or of how you came to be adopted. You simply feel that an important part of your story has been forgotten and lost. Try as you might, you cannot re-connect with your roots. The question, 'Who am I, really?' nags at you and will not go away.

Then, one day, a foreign-looking visitor calls who introduces herself as a friend of your natural parents. She has a photograph of you as a baby with your parents before your adoption. She is able to tell you the story of your birth, which might be either happy or tragic. It might be a story of poverty, of parents struggling to feed all their children and sending a child for adoption in this country in order to survive. Or it might be a story of a family divided by war, separated in refugee camps and the baby rescued by aid workers. Or it might be a story of loss and of death, of a mother and baby abandoned by a faithless father when he learnt she was terminally ill. Whatever the story, it fills in the blank and gives you a new sense of where you have come from, and consequently of who you are, alongside the identity you have received from your adoptive family.

Now consider these scenarios with the Bible playing the main part. Think of the Bible as the mirror in which you see your true self after years of fantasy, denial and forgetfulness. Think of the Bible as the story which reveals your true identity after years of searching and of feeling that something is missing.

Imagine how you would feel if the Bible could do that for you. Imagine how your attitude towards it might change. Imagine how you might read it differently.

Suppose the church was the community of remembered faces and reconnected identities. Ponder how it could ensure that the Bible performed this function of reminding and connecting within the community and was not neglected or used for some other purpose.

Closing Prayer

Lord, your word of life wakens our hearts from the sleep of forgetfulness:
Give us ears to hear your word and hearts to receive it,
that we may know who we truly are,
and be called from restlessness and wandering
to acceptance and fellowship
in the service of your Son, Jesus Christ our Lord. Amen.

Action

If you read on in Nehemiah 8 you will see how the people instituted a special festival to help them remember their identity. In what ways do we celebrate the core memories of the Christian community? Devise an act of worship or community event designed to highlight the distinctive nature of the Christian family and to help individuals to feel that they are part of it.

4
The Authority of Scripture: 2 Timothy 3.10–4.5

Introductory Comment

The word 'authority' rings the wrong bells nowadays for many people. We do not like 'authority' because we associate it with the misuse of power. At a deep level, none of us like being told what to do. For people who enjoy an unprecedented degree of personal freedom it is truly astonishing how often the theme of individual freedom versus repressive authority still features in our popular culture. Countless books, films, songs and television shows proceed as if the sources of authority in our society (from parents to politicians, social workers to teachers, and from kings to clergy) deserve only our deepest suspicion and can never work for our benefit!

Nevertheless, you may be able to think of representatives of authority whom you welcome and respect. It might be the inspiring teacher whose passion for her subject is infectious. It might be the financial adviser who tells you what kind of mortgage is best for you. It might be the policeman who keeps the traffic moving. There are many different kinds of authority, many of them wholly positive, but all open to abuse. When we talk about the 'authority of Scripture' the same ambiguity applies, and nowhere more so than in this passage.

In this letter the ageing apostle Paul is giving advice to the young church leader Timothy. Many scholars question whether Paul really was the author of this letter, but whoever it was had a deep concern to safeguard sound teaching in the churches, and to keep their faith firmly based on the Scriptures. The passage underlines the special authority of the Bible, which stems from the claim that it is 'able to make you wise for salvation through faith in Jesus Christ.' In other words, the Bible has authority to reveal and to put us in contact with the God and Father of our Lord Jesus Christ.

This is also the only place in the Bible where it is claimed that Scripture is inspired by God (literally, 'God-breathed'). Consequently, the relationship between the divine and human authors of Scripture has been much debated as have the implications of inspiration. For example, does 'inspiration' mean that God dictated the text, or that Scripture is inspired in the same way as the works of Shakespeare, or that inspiration guarantees the factual accuracy of the Bible? The Bible writers themselves do not show much interest in these questions. For our purposes, the significance of the claim to inspiration is that it conveys the idea that the Bible is a gift which God himself has provided. It has authority because it is personal to God and can therefore reveal him to us.

THE AUTHORITY OF SCRIPTURE: 2 TIMOTHY 3.10–4.5

Preparatory Prayer
Father God,
you breathe life through the Scriptures to make us wise for salvation:
As we read your word, send your Holy Spirit into our hearts
that our faith may be quickened,
our understanding deepened,
and our wills strengthened to serve the living Lord, Jesus Christ. Amen.

Questions for Discussion
1. How do you feel when somebody tells you what to do? Why might it depend on the person exercising authority? Do you find the authority of Jesus more palatable than that of other authorities?
2. Consider what kind of authority might be exercised by each of the following:

    An Ordnance Survey map
    A letter from your lover
    An article in the *Daily Mail*
    A Statute passed by Act of Parliament
    A memo from your boss asking you to do something
    Hymns Ancient and Modern

    Which one is most truthful? In the Bible, how might the authority of a psalm differ from that of an epistle, or a parable, or one of the prophets?
3. Verse 16 says, 'All Scripture is inspired by God.' What do you think this means, and what difference does your answer make to the way you actually read the Bible?
4. In what circumstances might the authority of the Bible be misused? Are you comfortable with it being used in 'teaching, correcting, rebuking and training' (v 16)? Has there ever been an occasion when you acted in obedience to Scripture even though it was against your natural inclination?

Meditation
Our Lord Jesus Christ said, 'If you love me, keep my commandments; happy are those who hear the word of God and keep it.' Hear then these commandments which God has given to his people, and take them to heart.

I am the Lord your God: you shall have no other gods but me.
You shall love the Lord your God with all your heart, with all your soul, with all your mind and with all your strength.
Amen. Lord, have mercy

ATTENDING TO SCRIPTURE

You shall not make for yourself any idol.
God is spirit, and those who worship him must worship in spirit and in truth.
Amen. Lord, have mercy

You shall not dishonour the name of the Lord your God.
You shall worship him with awe and reverence.
Amen. Lord, have mercy

Remember the Lord's day and keep it holy.
Christ is risen from the dead: set your minds on things that are above, not on things that are on the earth.
Amen. Lord, have mercy

Honour your father and mother.
Live as servants of God; honour everyone; love the family of believers.
Amen. Lord, have mercy

You shall not commit murder.
Be reconciled to your brother or sister; overcome evil with good.
Amen. Lord, have mercy

You shall not commit adultery.
Know that your body is a temple of the Holy Spirit.
Amen. Lord, have mercy

You shall not steal.
Be honest in all that you do and care for those in need.
Amen. Lord, have mercy

You shall not be a false witness.
Let everyone speak the truth.
Amen. Lord, have mercy

You shall not covet anything which belongs to your neighbour.
Remember the words of the Lord Jesus: It is more blessed to give than to receive.
Love your neighbour as yourself, for love is the fulfilling of the law.
Amen. Lord, have mercy

(From the *Alternative Service Book 1980*—adapted)

THE AUTHORITY OF SCRIPTURE: 2 TIMOTHY 3.10-4.5

Closing Prayer
Almighty and everlasting God,
increase in us your gift of faith;
that, forsaking what lies behind
and reaching out to that which is before,
we may run the way of your commandments
and win the crown of everlasting joy;
through Jesus Christ our Lord. Amen.   (From *Common Worship*)

Action
Ask several people outside the church what kind of authority they respect. Invite them to suggest how the church might present its teaching so that it attracts assent.

5
Meditating on God's Word: Psalm 1

Comment

The psalms provide a rich source of raw material for meditation, and as such they can take us directly into the presence of God. They are intimate, personal and express a very wide range of emotions from ecstasy to despair. Precisely because they are so intensely human and honest they are easy to identify with, even though the awareness of God which they display is exceptional.

The psalms are a very special part of God's word because they help us to speak to God, as well as *vice versa*. They embody the two-way conversation that is implicit in all Scripture. In this conversation we read Scripture as God's word to us, and then turn the words around as appropriate and allow them to become our words to God. This pattern reflects the dynamic of the Christian faith in which God both takes the initiative in speaking his word to us and also makes possible our response through the help of the Holy Spirit.

Psalm 1 is the gateway to the rest of the Psalter, and introduces us to some of the major themes that recur, not least the theme of devotion to God and his law. Christian meditation is a skill that needs to be learned and practised. Unlike the meditative techniques used in some eastern religions, Christian meditation does not involve emptying the mind of conscious thought. On the contrary, we give the words of Scripture our focussed and careful attention. We attend to God in the Scriptures with our whole being, conscripting our emotions, imagination, conscience and will to the task as well as our intellect.

The verses are read slowly, carefully, and prayerfully. Selected words and phrases may be repeated, or even memorized so that they can take root in our hearts and provide nourishment over a period of time. We are trying to follow the guidance of Martin Luther, who advised: 'Pause at every verse of Scripture and shake, as it were, every bough of it, that if possible some fruit at least may drop down.' The ultimate goal, astonishing in its simplicity and boldness, is for us to grow in experience of, intimacy with, and surrender to the living God.

Preparatory Prayer

Blessed Lord,
who caused all holy Scriptures to be written for our learning:
Help us so to hear them, to read, mark, learn and inwardly digest them

that, through patience, and the comfort of your holy word,
we may embrace and hold fast the hope of everlasting life,
which you have given us through our Saviour Jesus Christ. Amen.

(From *Common Worship*)

Questions for Discussion
1. Do you have any experience of meditating upon God's word? If you do, how do you personally approach the task of scriptural meditation?
2. The central image in Psalm 1 is that of the tree planted by streams of water (v 3). What things nourish your faith and keep it growing and fruitful? How do you look after the 'roots' of your faith?
3. Consider the distinction between the person who delights in the Lord and 'the wicked.' Setting aside for a moment your own ideas of who might be 'righteous' and who might be 'wicked,' consider what the psalm suggests are the hallmarks of each. When the psalmist talks about 'the wicked,' what sort of people does he have in mind, and how judgmental is he being? How comfortable are you with these distinctions?
4. The image of the tree yielding its fruit in due season suggests a need for patience, attentiveness, a confidence in future growth and a discipline of regular tending and watering. How helpful do you find this as a pattern for the growth of your faith?

Meditation
Picture in your mind a seed. It looks small, hard, uninteresting, dead. Imagine the sower or gardener scattering the seed so that it lands in all kinds of different places. It falls upon rocky ground, on hard paths, amongst weeds, on cultivated soil. Imagine the seed struggling to grow. There is too much or too little water, too much or too little sun. The seed is vulnerable and easily lost. Yet it is also full of life. It grows in unlikely places, in deserts and on cliff faces, in shade and in marsh. It spreads its roots in search of food. It wills to live and to grow. It pushes up between the cracks in the soil. It breaks up the obstacles which get in its way. Its shoots appear through concrete and mortar. It gradually grows to maturity, flowers, and produces more seeds.

Imagine the seed of God's word being sown in your heart. Where does it land? In what crevices of your soul does it lodge? Consider the things which snatch it away, or choke it, or prevent it from growing. The busyness and lack of time. The forgetfulness. The anxieties. The scorn or indifference of others. The sin to which you cling. The lack of space. The distracting weeds competing for attention. The impatience which expects too much too soon.

Will the seed wither and die? Or will it catch hold and grow? It needs tending and weeding, watering and feeding. Roots begin to appear, gradually reaching out into every part of your life. You experience it as a source of energy and renewal, giving to you rather than taking from you. This seed feeds you and nourishes you, giving your life a structure and purpose, shaping you and filling you with the goodness of God. Imagine blossoming from within as the seed of God's word matures in your heart. Imagine the growth pains as the shoots break up the hard crust around your heart and you begin to grow in ways you had not planned. Imagine what fruit you might bear; the things you are gifted in, the qualities you have to offer and the love you can share. Imagine such fruits growing and multiplying, becoming an abundance beyond your dreams. Imagine becoming an object of grace, strength and beauty in the garden of the Lord, because there is space in your heart for the seed of God's word to grow. He who has ears to hear, let him hear.

Closing Prayer

Teach me, Lord, to feed on your word and be trained by your promises. I am slow to learn, and like to think I know what is best. My heart is tangled and unruly, but you are the gardener who can make me grow straight and tall. Weed out my fear and self-loathing. Prune my pride and my self-deception. Let your word be to me a source of water and life in a dry land. Let me cling to the rod of your promises. May my spiritual roots penetrate the truths of your word, that they might hold me and become part of me. Let me be ready for the times of testing, when things go wrong and my plans fail. Let me withstand the times of drought, when my spirit is hard and you seem far away. Nourish me with your word, that little by little my life may bear fruit that is pleasing in all seasons. By your grace, let me remain in Jesus and his words remain in me, in order that I, even I, may be part of the Lord's planting, for the display of his splendour. Amen.

Action

What sort of spiritual fruit do you hope your life might yield? Is there one practical step you can take to move that desire towards reality? Tell someone what you have decided to do.

6
Christ the Key to the Scriptures: Acts 8.26–40

Comment

Most Christians have had the experience of reading a passage from the Bible and of being left wondering, 'What was that all about?' It is reassuring to discover examples in Scripture of people who try to read Scripture but find that for them also it remains a 'closed' book.

There may be various reasons for this. We may lack knowledge of the historical context of a passage. The subject matter may be too alien or technical in nature. But often the reason may be spiritual. Much of the Bible was written by people of faith for the benefit of other people of faith, and it needs to be read in that light. The impression a passage makes on us will depend to some degree upon the level of spiritual expectation and hunger we bring to it. In terms of the parable of the sower, much depends upon the kind of soil in which the word of God lands. This passage from Acts is a good example.

The Ethiopian eunuch is a surprisingly contemporary Bible reader. As a senior civil servant from a far country he is at once intelligent, unfamiliar with the Bible and yet spiritually hungry. He is also very much on the outside looking in on what seems to be an insiders' book. He feels that the text should speak to him personally but is unable to make much sense out of it. (One intriguing suggestion is that he was reading Isaiah because of chapter 56.3–8, with its promises of inclusion among God's people and an 'everlasting name' even for eunuchs and foreigners).

Philip helps the Ethiopian to approach the Isaiah text with an awareness of Jesus and a desire to know him. The Ethiopian is then able to bring that knowledge to the text, and it speaks to him with real power and illumination. The world of the text and the world of the reader need to be brought into contact with each other, and often this will only happen if the text is read in the light of the gospel and with some degree of faith already present.

The Ethiopian Orthodox Church today has a tradition that it owes its foundation to the incident recorded in this passage. It is a powerful reminder of the far-reaching consequences that can arise as we bring our present-day concerns alongside those of the Bible and relate them to each other in the light of the gospel.

A Rough Guide to Biblical Interpretation

It is clear from this passage that the word of God does not automatically speak to the reader, but that there needs to be a process of interpretation before the reader can connect with the text and hear it speak in the present. In chapter 1, I suggested that as a bare minimum only two principles need to be observed, namely to read the Bible in the context both of faith and the believing community. We might develop that to offer a marginally more sophisticated process of interpretation involving the following three questions:

i) In the original historical setting, what did the writer of the text intend to say? In Acts 8 the Ethiopian asks this of the Isaiah passage when he says, 'Who is the prophet talking about, himself or someone else?' (v 34). Asking this question helps to ground the process in reality and stops us from making a text mean anything we want it to mean.
ii) In the light of the gospel, what does the church think the passage says? This question acknowledges that we are not the first to read the text, and that we read it as part of a community of faith. Philip answers this question in v 35 by starting 'with that very passage of Scripture' and relating it to 'the good news about Jesus.'
iii) In the light of my own circumstances and experience, what does the passage say to me? This question draws the reader into the passage and invites a personal response to it leading to practical action. We do not know exactly how the passage from Isaiah spoke to the Ethiopian, but it clearly made a deep impression because he responded by asking for baptism.

We could add further steps, for example asking about the historical events of which the biblical narrative claims to be a report, or perhaps about how the passage relates to the world beyond the church. We might also want to consider the biblical context (how the passage fits into the rest of the Bible), and such issues as the type of writing represented by the passage (its 'genre'). Such complexities take us beyond the scope of this work, and it is enough to acknowledge that I am offering here only a very basic guide.

Preparatory Prayer
   Almighty Father,
   whose Son our Saviour Jesus Christ is the light of the world:
   May your people, illumined by your word and sacraments,
   shine with the radiance of his glory,
   that he may be known, worshipped and obeyed to the ends of the earth;
   for he is alive and reigns, now and for ever. Amen.
                                            (From *Common Worship*)

Questions for Discussion
1. Philip plays a key role in helping the Ethiopian towards a deeper understanding of the passage he was reading. In what ways do you receive

help from the community of the church in understanding the Bible and hearing the word of God?
2. When the Ethiopian asks Philip to explain the passage from Isaiah, Philip 'told him the good news about Jesus' (v 35). How does the gospel illuminate the passage from Isaiah, and how does Isaiah help your understanding of the gospel? You may wish to look at Isaiah 52.13–53.12 in its entirety.
3. Consider the different roles played in this passage by Spirit, word and sacrament. Should we expect to find those roles in a similar way in the church today?
4. How can your church help people today to connect with the gospel and discover that it still addresses their present condition and concerns?

Meditation

O God, you are my God, earnestly I seek you. My soul thirsts for you, my spirit hungers for your truth. I come to your word, O Lord, eagerly searching to find food for my soul. Like the Ethiopian I believe I may put my hope in your word, but like him I read the holy Scriptures and find that a veil hangs before my eyes. I devour your promises but cannot digest them. My mind is darkened. My understanding is shallow. Your word rests exposed like a seed on the hardened surface of my heart, unable to break through.

Have mercy upon me, O Lord. Lighten my darkness with the torch of your truth. As I read your word may the same Holy Spirit who inspired the ancient writers illuminate my poor mind and open the eyes of my heart. May that same Holy Spirit who guided Philip to the Ethiopian lead me into the company of pilgrims more wise, more faithful, and further along the way than I. Grant me humility to admit my blindness. Grant me grace to learn from others.

Thank you, Lord, for the promise that your word makes wise the simple. Give me the simplicity to listen. Grant me stillness of heart that I may hear. Make me attentive to the whispering dance between your word, your Spirit and your church, that I may be caught up with joy in its steps. Will you truly speak, Lord, even to me? The word that goes out from your mouth, O my God, will surely not return to you empty, but will accomplish what you desire. As for me, my soul will be satisfied as with the finest of foods. How sweet are your words to my taste, O Lord, sweeter than honey to my mouth!

Action

Create a visual display to go in your church giving examples of how biblical passages can speak to present-day concerns—for example, Leviticus 25 and the Jubilee 2000/Drop the Debt campaign.

7
Entering God's Story: Luke 24.13-49[1]

Comment

It is difficult not to tell stories. When we are asked, 'How has your day been?' we try to impose some sort of narrative shape on the otherwise tangled and chaotic thoughts, conversations and experiences which have made up our day. The stories we tell about ourselves say a lot to others about who we think we are. When you meet someone new, which bit of your story do you tell her first? You might start with your family, or your work, or your childhood, or your interests. Each of us will shape our story in a different way.

In its overall scheme, the Bible relates the story of God and his world. It is not a neat and orderly story, for its different chapters are not all chronological, neither are they all narrative in structure. It involves many different writers and characters, is told from many different points of view, and includes episodes occurring hundreds of years apart. At the beginning there are two different accounts of the creation. At the end there are glimpses of creation healed and completed in the new heaven and new earth. Throughout the story God is the main character; and the plot revolves around God's complex relationship with humanity, focussed on Israel, then on Jesus, and finally on the church.

In Luke 24 the two travellers on the road to Emmaus were familiar with the broad shape of the biblical story and the role of Israel within it. As followers of Jesus they thought they knew how the story of Israel's Messiah would work out. It was a story which should have had a happy and triumph-ant ending ('We had hoped that he was the one who was going to redeem Israel' v 21). Instead, the events of Good Friday had turned the triumph into tragedy and they were left bewildered and disorientated, unable to figure out how they could have got the story so wrong, and unable to see the consequences for their own lives. With the death of the Messiah it seemed there was to be no liberation from foreign oppression, no final end to the exile, no renewal of the covenant, and no new beginning for God's people.

As the two disciples go their despondent way, the presence of Jesus himself helps them to fit together the different pieces of the puzzle in a new and unexpected way. Only then can they once more connect the big story of God and his world to the story of Jesus and see their own lives as part of that

---

[1] The basic structure of this study owes its inspiration to a Bible reading given by Tom Wright to the Evangelical Anglican Leaders' Conference at Westminster Hall in 1996.

ENTERING GOD'S STORY: LUKE 24.13-49

story and a continuation of it. Jesus himself says as much when he addresses the gathered disciples in the upper room later that evening and tells them, 'You are witnesses of these things' (v 48).

Preparatory Prayer
   Father in heaven,
   you are the God to whom the Law,
   the Prophets and the Psalms bear witness:
   Send down upon us the Spirit of the risen Lord,
   that in his presence our minds might be opened to understand your word,
   our hearts burn within us,
   and our lives become pages upon which the tale of Christ's love is told.
   Amen.

Questions for Discussion
1. Turn to your neighbour and for two minutes tell him or her about yourself. What are the most important parts of your story, and why?
2. How does the passage summarize the story of God and his world? How did Cleopas and his friend get the story wrong, and how did Jesus correct them?
3. 'Then their eyes were opened and they recognized him' (v 31). Compare this verse with Genesis 3.7 and consider its significance. Are you aware of any important moments of recognition in your life which helped you better to understand yourself and your place in the world?
4. How is it that a deeper understanding of Jesus' story leads the disciples to a deeper understanding of their own story (vv 44–49)? Do you have any sense of your story being connected to God's story? What might strengthen that feeling of sharing in God's story? How can the church help?
5. In reality we live in the light not just of the Christian story but of many other stories or fragments of stories, each offering its own ideals and values. What rival 'stories' can you see in the advertisements, films, magazines and songs which surround us in Western society? What might it mean for us to be Christ's witnesses (v 48) in such a context?

Meditation
   Picture in your mind those two disciples on the road to Emmaus. It is the afternoon, and the hot sun is beginning to go down. The road is hard and dusty, the journey long, and the mood despondent. Having thrown in their lot with Jesus, and having been convinced that he was the Messiah who would rescue their nation, Cleopas and his friend have had their dream shattered. Their hopes, so recently high, have turned to despair. God seems completely

absent. He has let them down, and they do not know where to turn. They cannot make sense of the death of Jesus.

Now picture yourself walking alongside them. Imagine bringing with you your own, very contemporary doubts and disappointments. Think of the disillusionment and cynicism which clouds our times. After two world wars, the Holocaust, countless ethnic conflicts and the rise of international terrorism, it seems the world is no closer to its dream of achieving peace. After Hiroshima and Chernobyl, thalidomide and global warming, biological weapons and the cloning of human embryos, we no longer trust in the benign purity of science and technology. With the gap between rich and poor widening, with a million unemployed accepted without question, and with the unmoveable burden of Third World debt, we no longer look to the markets for salvation. We are finding it harder to believe in the possibility of personal happiness. With the more economically advanced countries reporting unparalleled levels of addictive behaviour, AIDS, depression, divorce, stress-related illness, and violence, it seems that even for the privileged the pursuit of happiness can turn out to be a will o' the wisp.

The stories we used to tell to make sense of our situation and to guide our hopes and aspirations have broken down and we are left with the fragments, pieces of wreckage we still cling to for lack of a more coherent alternative. Some call for a return to the certainties of the past, some seek ever more refined pleasures to escape from the realities of the present, some turn to 'green' spirituality, some think the answer to mass poverty and injustice is to insulate ourselves from such uncomfortable things and pretend that they are not our problem, while some claim there is no point in looking for a new story at all because all stories are meaningless.

Think also of your own, more personal disappointments. The ideals betrayed. The relationships neglected or broken. The responsibilities shunned. The hurts received and resented. The sight of others more successful, more content, but less deserving. The sheer unfairness of so much of life. Where is God? Why does not he do something? Why does he allow it to happen? Why do I find it so difficult to make sense of his part in my story?

A figure appears alongside you. 'What are you talking about?,' he asks. You explain why you are so despondent, and about how all your dreams have come to nothing. Your companion gently rebukes you and says, 'How foolish you are, and how slow of heart to believe all that the prophets have spoken! Do you not realize that those who follow Christ must suffer with him? Do you not realize that this is the pattern, repeated throughout the Bible, by which God overcomes the sin of the world? God's purpose is not to help you to avoid the pain of the world, but to share it and to heal it by his love shown through you. The Christ has suffered and entered his glory, and has shown you the way to glory yourself. It is for you now to take his part in the drama of God and his world and to live it out. You are to offer to others around you the story of the Creator God and his Son, the story of love overcoming sin, the story of death and resurrection, the story of repentance and forgiveness. It is time for you to step into God's grand drama and to play your part under the guidance of the Holy Spirit, improvising from the script of the Scriptures to make Christ's role your own. You are to offer that story to the world by what you say, by the way you worship, and by the way you live. You are my witnesses.'

So saying, the Lord sits down beside you at table. He takes bread, gives thanks, breaks it and shares it with you. And as you receive it, as you eat and are nourished by his hand, your eyes suddenly are opened, and you recognize him.

Action
Draw up an agenda for your church of things it might realistically do to make its story reflect God's story more faithfully. Discuss your agenda with members of the church council.

Closing Prayer
Almighty God,
We thank you for the gift of your holy word.
May it be a lantern to our feet,
a light upon our paths,
and a strength to our lives.
Take us and use us to love and serve all people
in the power of the Holy Spirit
and in the name of your Son,
Jesus Christ our Lord. Amen.   (From *Common Worship*)

8
For Further Reading

General
Bible Reading for Amateurs, Michael Green (Hodder & Stoughton, 1999)
Can Balaam's Ass Speak Today? Walter Moberly (Grove Biblical booklet B 10)
Imagining the Gospels, Kathy Galloway (SPCK, 1988)
Invitation to the Bible, Stephen Barton (SPCK, 1997)
Lo and Behold!, Trevor Dennis (SPCK, 1991)
Meditating upon God's Word, Peter Toon (DLT, 1988)
Praying the Bible: An Introduction to Lectio Divina, Mariano Magrassi (The Liturgical Press, 1998)
Praying the Psalms, John Goldingay (Grove Spirituality booklet S 44)

Bible Study Notes
Bible Reading Fellowship
Guidelines (Straightforward commentary on passages without application)
New Daylight (Commentary with some devotional material)

Crusade for World Revival
Every Day with Jesus (Inspirational, with an emphasis on the Holy Spirit)
YP's (Accessible and practical, for teenagers)

International Bible Reading Association
Light for our Path (Good for new Bible readers starting out)
Words for Today (Relates the Bible to contemporary issues. Both this and *Light for our Path* bring a refreshing international perspective)

St Matthias Press
Explore (Challenging and alert to the demands of modern Christian living)
The Icthus File (Aimed at teenagers. Pithy, relevant and good fun)

Scripture Union
Closer to God (Inspirational and devotional, including suggested responses)
Daily Bread (Middle of the road devotional notes)
Encounter with God (Scholarly, systematic commentary with brief devotional suggestions)
One Up (Interactive studies for teens, without any commentary)
Snap Shots (Simple notes for children)